hand-made habitats

# BIRD

## Paul Wright
### Photographs by Robert Pickett

**A & C Black · London**

First published 1992
A & C Black (Publishers) Limited
35 Bedford Row, London WC1R 4JH

ISBN 0-7136-3548-7

A CIP catalogue record for this book
is available from the British Library.

## Acknowledgements

Illustrations by Patricia Newell of John Martin and
Artists Limited.

Photographs by Robert Pickett, except for: p4b Tony
Wilson-Bligh, Papillio; p5t Philip Marazzi, Papillio; p5b
Robert Marsh, Papillio; p18 (inset) Chris Beddall,
Papillio; p19b Clive Druett, Papillio; p23 Barrie Watts;
p25t Dennis Johnson, Papillio; p25b Robert Marsh,
Papillio; p26t Chris Beddall, Papillio; p26b Eric Gilbert,
Papillio; p28 Jamie Harron, Papillio; p29 Pat Gerrold,
Papillio; pp30/31 Michael Maconachie, Papillio; p30b
Dennis Johnson, Papillio.

The author and publisher would like to thank the staff and
pupils of Bolshaw Primary School, Bredbury Green Junior
School, Lum Head Primary School and Eardley Junior
School whose help and co-operation made this book possible.

Filmset by Rowland Phototypesetting Limited,
Bury St Edmunds, Suffolk
Printed in Italy by Imago

# Contents

| Bird | Beak | Likely food |
|------|------|-------------|
| Blue tit | small, sharp, straight | insects |
| Kestrel | strong, sharp, hooked | animals, birds |
| Robin | | |
| Thrush | | |
| Magpie | | |

# Bird habitats

Have you ever noticed how many different kinds of birds live all around you? Whatever the season, whether you live in the busiest city or the quietest countryside, you'll find thousands of these beautiful creatures feeding, singing, breeding and showing off wherever you look.

**A Robin**

**A House Sparrow** ▲

Some, like Swifts and Martins, arrive covered in desert dust every spring to build nests under house eaves and chase insects over meadows and ponds. Others, like the Redwings and Fieldfares, fly away when spring arrives after the cold winter. Lots more, like the Robin and the Wren, stay all year long, whatever the weather.

With a little careful planning, you can attract many different kinds of birds into your garden or school grounds where they will feed or perhaps even nest. You may already have noticed Sparrows, Blackbirds, Starlings and Thrushes. But there are other species too, such as Black-headed Gulls and Wagtails, which will visit the habitats you build for them.

It doesn't matter where you live – with a bit of encouragement Magpies and Jays will drop in on built-up city areas, while Pigeons, Blue Tits and Greenfinches are frequent visitors to most places.

**A Song Thrush** ▲

These days, most birds are finding it harder to survive, because people are destroying the hedges and trees which birds rely on for food and shelter. By building habitats for birds, you will not only be able to study these creatures close-up, you will also be providing them with essential places where they can feed and nest.

◀ **Swallows on telephone wires**

# Bird-tables

Birds spend most of their time and energy finding enough food to survive, especially in winter. A good way to attract interesting birds is to provide food for them.

## Build a bird-table

**You will need:**

a piece of ply wood measuring about 40 cm by 50 cm (marine ply is the best wood to use)

some nails

a drill

a length of thick cord

wood to make the edging strip measuring about 1 cm by 1 cm by 200 cm

a saw

a hammer

Cut two 30 cm-long pieces of edging strip and two 40 cm-long pieces. Nail them along the edges of the piece of ply wood. Leave a gap in each corner to brush stale food off the table.

Drill two holes on opposite sides of the table, each about 4 cm from the edge. Thread the cord through the holes so that the bird-table hangs from the cord. Tie the ends of the cord firmly to make a strong knot. Use the loops of cord to hang the table from the branch of a tree.

You could make a free-standing bird-table by using hinges to fix the table top to a post.

Think carefully when you decide where to put the bird-table you've made. Try to position the table in a place where you can see it from indoors. Choose somewhere quiet, where you'll be able to watch the feeding birds without disturbing them. Make sure there are no sneaky approaches for cats!

Put food out once or twice a day from November right through until the beginning of May. You'll find that birds will visit the table regularly, and soon come to depend on it. Many of them will survive through the winter on the food that they find on bird-tables like yours. If this food supply stops before spring arrives, birds may die. So try to put something out for them every day if you can.

# Food for birds

Most kitchen leftovers, such as breadcrumbs, bacon rinds, apples and potatoes make good food for birds. You can buy special wild bird feed from pet shops, too.

Make sure that you clean off any scraps of old food before you put fresh food on to the bird-table. Don't give the birds mouldy food, or desiccated coconut, as these can be harmful to them. Provide a supply of fresh water for the birds to drink every day.

Some birds have special diets. For instance, you can attract seed eaters like Finches to your table by putting out sunflower seeds for them. Use a reference guide to help you find out which foods will attract different sorts of unusual birds. There is a list of useful guides on page 32.

Try out your own test to find out which foods each bird prefers. Mark out a grid or put down some hoops on an area of ground and use each section to test a particular kind of food. Note down every bird that visits each section of the grid.

|  | Cheese | Bread | Fruit | Nuts | Bacon rind |
|---|---|---|---|---|---|
|  |  |  |  | ✓ | ✓ |
| Blue tit |  |  |  |  |  |
| Great tit |  | ✓ |  |  |  |
| Sparrow |  |  |  |  |  |
| Robin |  |  |  |  |  |
| Greenfinch |  |  |  |  |  |
| Starling |  |  |  |  |  |
| Blackbird | ✓ | ✓ |  |  |  |
| Thrush |  |  |  |  |  |

You could vary the test to find out whether birds prefer brown bread to white, or apples to pears, or cheddar cheese to edam. Do some birds like cake more than bread? Does a Sparrow have a sweet beak?

Show the results of your survey on a graph. If you have a microcomputer you could use a database like 'Ourfacts' or 'List Explorer' to sort out the information for you.

Blue Tits and Great Tits are very clever feeders and great acrobats. They can hang upside down to eat and sometimes even do tricks or solve problems. You can buy special feeders for Tits, but you can make them quite simply yourself using everyday materials.

## Make a bird cake

**You will need:**

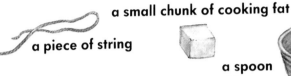

a small chunk of cooking fat

a piece of string

a spoon

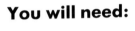

an empty yoghurt pot

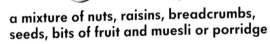

a mixture of nuts, raisins, breadcrumbs, seeds, bits of fruit and muesli or porridge

a bowl

Thread the string through the top of the yoghurt pot. Put the mixture of dry food scraps into a bowl. Melt the cooking fat and allow it to cool. While it is still liquid, pour it into the bowl and stir. Press the mixture into the pot so that it clings to the string. When the mixture has set, hang the pot upside down from your bird-table for Tits to feed on.

Use a needle and cotton to thread bacon rinds or unshelled peanuts together and hang them from a branch or a corner of the bird-table. Tits will enjoy hanging upside down to eat them.

Some birds prefer to eat scraps from the ground. If you scatter food around the bird-table, make sure that you remove any leftovers each evening. If food is left on the ground, there is a danger that it will attract rats and mice.

Water is as important to birds as it is to us. Like us, birds need clean water to drink and to bathe in. Make sure that you provide a fresh supply of water near your bird-table. Choose a place which won't be disturbed by cats. You could use a margarine tub or even an old washing up bowl. Sink the container into the ground before you fill it with water.

You could use a similar container or an old dustbin lid to make a bird-bath but you must make sure that the birds cannot tip it up. Check the bath each day to make sure that it's clean and the water in it is fresh.

# Birdwatching

You will need to get as close as possible to the feeding birds if you are going to observe them properly. It's important to bear this in mind when you're planning where to position your bird-table (look back at page 6).

If you can see your bird-table from a room indoors, you can make a hide or screen. When you stand behind a hide, the birds outside will not be able to see you watching them.

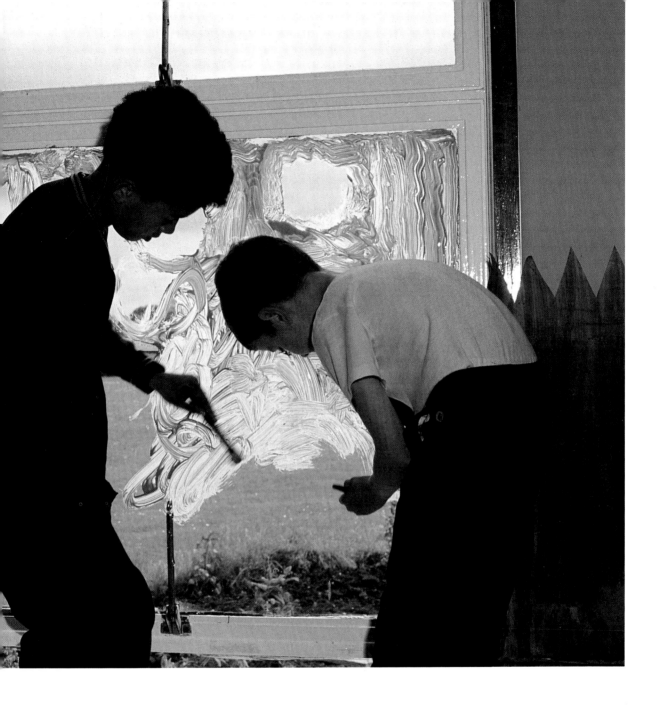

All you need to make a hide is green or brown window
paint. Paint the window nearest to the bird-table at least as
high as the tallest person who will be using the hide. Make
sure that you have permission before you start painting.
Leave several openings in the paint for you to look through.

If you can't see your bird-table from indoors, there are other ways of getting close to it without the birds noticing. One good way is to make an outdoor hide.

Fix two posts into the ground about two metres apart and seven or eight metres away from the bird-table. (You could use tree trunks if there are suitable trees in the area.) Tie a length of string between the two posts or tree trunks. Then drape a piece of dark material (an old curtain is ideal) over the string. Cut slits in the material to make eyeholes to look through.

When you've finished making the hide, leave it for a few days to let the birds get used to it being there.

Try to approach the table from behind the hide and wait quietly for the birds to continue feeding.

A pair of binoculars or a telescope makes birdwatching much easier and more exciting. If you haven't got a pair yourself, ask around to see if someone can lend you a pair.

The best binoculars for birdwatching are not necessarily the biggest and most expensive. It takes a bit of practice to focus binoculars, but after a while it gets much easier.

To focus a pair of binoculars, look through the eyepieces at an object which is about 20 metres away. Close your right eye and turn the big wheel in the middle of the binoculars until the object is in sharp focus. Close your left eye and open your right eye. Turn the small wheel on the right eyepiece until the object is in focus. Then open both your eyes.

# Identifying birds

As soon as you start bird-watching you'll want to find out more about the many different kinds or species of birds that visit your garden or school grounds.

Most of these birds change their plumage or feathers as they mature, and at different times of the year, too. Many species also have different plumage for males and females. At first this can make it very difficult to identify some of the birds that you see. It doesn't take long to get the hang of it though.

You will need a good identification guide or 'key' to help you. But don't start by looking in a guide when you want to identify a bird. This will take so long that the bird will fly away before you manage to identify it. Try to 'take a photograph' with your memory. This will help you to identify the bird later when you have time to look it up in a guide.

Use a fact sheet like this one to record your observations while you are looking at the bird.

Bird Identification Sheet

How big is it?

What is its main colour?

Any other colours?

What colour are its legs?

What shape is its beak?

How long is its tail?

What shape is its tail?

What is it doing?

Are there any other birds with it?

Draw a quick sketch:

The information you record will make it much easier to identify the bird when you're using a reference guide. Be careful, though, as these will often have pictures of rare birds, or birds from other countries, that you will probably never see.

# Make a bird garden

Most birds depend upon trees, hedges and plants for food and shelter.

**A Chaffinch** ▲

You can introduce trees and plants into your garden or school grounds, and make a habitat that birds will choose to stay in all year round. A bird garden can be any size; you can even grow one in a concrete or tarmac yard.

When you're planning your bird garden, think carefully about what to include in it. Here are some ideas:

● A range of possible nesting sites such as shrubs, trees or nesting boxes.

● Clean water for birds to drink and bathe in. A pond would be ideal for this, but a bird-bath will do just as well.

● A bird-table in a quiet position that can be easily observed.

● A variety of different plants.

● Good places for birds to sing from – perhaps tree branches or posts hammered into the ground.

● Is vandalism likely to be a problem? If it is, you can plant thorny hedges of Hawthorn and Pyracantha which are more resistant to vandals.

When you're choosing plants for your bird garden, try to avoid any foreign species. This is because plants from abroad will not provide suitable food for many of the insects or birds that you're trying to attract.

A wildflower seed mix sown in the ground or under a hedgerow will help to bring birds into the garden. You can buy wildflower seeds quite cheaply from garden centres, but it's often cheaper to buy them through the post. There is a list of addresses to write to on page 32. Plants such as Currant bushes, Sunflowers, Wheat and Barley all attract birds which eat their fruits or seeds.

You can make a bird garden on a patch of concrete or tarmac. Grow plants in pots, window boxes, tubs and old tyres filled with soil or compost. Many building sites and wastelands are homes to all sorts of birds and other creatures.

◀ **A Starling**

# Nesting boxes

You can help visiting birds find a place to nest and breed by planting trees and shrubs and by putting up nesting boxes in suitable places.

## Make a nesting box

**You will need:**

**a piece of wood measuring about 15 cm by 1 cm by 140 cm**

| 20cm | 15 cm | 15 cm | 25cm | 20 cm | 17 cm |
|---|---|---|---|---|---|
| SIDE | SIDE | FRONT | BACK | ROOF | FLOOR |
| 15cm | 20cm | 15cm | | | |

15cm

**a piece of roofing felt about 15 cm by 30 cm**

a drill

scissors

some nails

a vice

a hammer

a saw

Mark the measurements of each piece of the nesting box on the piece of wood and cut them out. Drill a hole in the front piece of the box. You may need some help with this – it can be fiddly.

If you want Blue Tits to use your box, make the hole in the front of it about 2.5 cm wide. If the hole is bigger than this, the box will be taken over by sparrows instead. Sparrows are good survivors and don't need much extra help.

Nail the sides of the box to the back, nail the front onto the box and nail the floor into place. Nail the piece of roofing felt to the roof and then nail this last piece into place. You could paint the box with wood preservative to protect the wood in wet weather.

When you're planning where to position your box you will first need to know which way the wind usually blows. This is called the prevailing wind direction. Make sure that the box doesn't face straight into the prevailing wind, or directly into the sun. Position it as high as you can on a building or a tree, so that it won't be disturbed.

It may take a while for the box to 'weather in', especially if you have used wood preservative. Avoid using creosote, because it has a very strong smell which birds do not like. Be patient, and watch your box when the spring comes. Don't disturb it though, as this could upset the birds and make them desert the nest.

## Different types of bird box

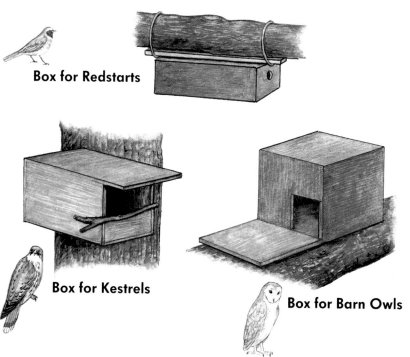

Box for Redstarts

Box for Kestrels

Box for Barn Owls

Different birds like different types of box. For example, Robins, Flycatchers and Wagtails like boxes with an open front. Try experimenting with different sizes and shapes of box.

# Finding out more

A Buzzard with its prey

You may have seen pictures of birds of prey, such as Buzzards, Hawks and Owls, eating mice, rabbits or other animals. In fact, nearly every bird will eat living animals if it gets the chance.

Blue Tits eat caterpillars, Sparrows eat worms and Thrushes eat snails. Most birds have a mixed diet that includes plants, seeds and animals. Only the birds of prey live mainly as predators, depending on living animals for their food.

The birds of prey eat smaller birds and mammals, which in turn eat insects and other minibeasts. Some of these eat other minibeasts (spiders eat flies, for example), but most minibeasts just eat plants.

All the creatures in a food chain like this one depend on plants for food. This is because plants are the only living things that can make their own food by using energy from the sun.

**sun**

**plants (e.g. oak tree)**

**insects
(e.g. caterpillar)**

**birds
(e.g. Long-tailed Tit)**

▲ A Long-tailed Tit with a
caterpillar which it has caught

**predators
(e.g. Sparrowhawk)**

A Sparrowhawk ▲

**Kestrel**

**vole vole vole vole**

**seeds seeds seeds seeds seeds seeds seeds**

**sunshine**

During the breeding season, a Tit family needs to eat hundreds of caterpillars every day. This means that there have to be lots more caterpillars than Tits.

The bigger a creature is, the more food it needs. It has to compete for food with other creatures of the same size, and, as there is not enough food to go round, not all of them will survive. So there will always be more caterpillars than Tits and more Tits than Sparrowhawks. This sort of pattern is called a food pyramid.

◀ Here is another food pyramid. Can you draw one of your own?

When a bird of prey eats a small animal, it either swallows the animal whole, or tears it up first with its strong, hooked beak. Once in the bird's stomach, the soft parts of the animal are digested. The rest is crushed together into a pellet which the bird then spits out.

Pellets are very interesting to examine. They can tell you exactly what the bird has eaten recently. They can also provide you with information about the food chain which the bird of prey belongs to.

An Australian Eagle

A Barn Owl in flight

# Examine an Owl pellet

Many birds produce pellets, but Owl pellets are the best to investigate because Owls don't tear up their food. Instead they swallow their prey whole.

## You will need:

container filled with water and disinfectant

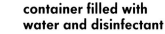

 pointed tweezers

 Owl pellets

hand lens or microscope

Soak the pellets in water with a little disinfectant added. Gently pull the pellet apart with the tweezers and use a hand lens or microscope to examine what you find. Look out for small bones, insect remains and fur.

Only birds of prey produce pellets to help you detect what they have eaten. But you can usually work out what other birds eat by looking at their wings, claws and beaks.

A Blue Tit

A Blue Tit has a small, delicate beak which acts like a sharp pair of tweezers to help it pick up peanuts and caterpillars. Blue Tits are quite good at grabbing bees, too. Once a Blue Tit has a bee in its grasp, it rubs the bee's sting off against a branch, and then sucks out the insides of the bee through the hole left by the sting.

This Puffin's beak is the perfect shape for holding its catch of sand eels. Kestrels have sharp, hooked beaks and strong neck muscles for tearing up their prey before eating it. Woodpeckers have strong, straight beaks which they use to bore holes in bark to reach the creatures hidden inside.

Look closely at the sorts of beaks that visit your bird table. What sorts of food do you think these birds eat?

▲ A Puffin holding its catch of sand eels

| Bird | Beak | Likely food |
|------|------|-------------|
| Blue tit | small, sharp, straight | insects |
| Kestrel | strong, sharp, hooked | animals, birds |
| Robin | | |
| Thrush | | |
| Magpie | | |

You could make a chart like this one and fill it in from your bird table observations.

# Birds and people

Sometimes birds can benefit from human activity. Pigeons grow fat in parks. Sparrows too, will pick over any morsel of food that people leave out for them. Martins nest under house eaves and Black-headed Gulls flock to rubbish tips. However, many of the things that people do make it harder for birds to survive.

Hedgerows provide important habitats for all sorts of birds. As well as giving shelter, hedges contain vital foods such as berries, fruits, seeds, shoots, insects and mammals. Hedges act like corridors, allowing birds like Jays and Tits to travel from one wood to another.

This Gannet was killed by oil pollution ▼

Yet every year hundreds of miles of hedges are cut down and replaced with wire fencing, or even not replaced at all. Where hedges remain they are often cut back in a way that destroys the taller hedgerow trees which many birds depend on.

On land, pesticides and agricultural chemicals may poison birds and other animals, or starve them by destroying the insects they eat. At sea, oil leaks and sewage kills thousands of birds every year.

There are things you can do to help the birds in your local area:

- grow plants that birds need for food, shelter and to nest in
- start an anti-litter campaign, or help to clean up a polluted river bank
- build nesting boxes

- provide food for them throughout the colder months of the year
- provide a supply of clean water for bathing and drinking all year round
- join a group like the Young Ornithologists' Club, which works to improve the welfare of birds, or an organisation like Friends of the Earth which works for a cleaner environment

# Index

## Useful addresses

*The Young Ornithologists' Club*
Royal Society for the Protection of Birds,
The Lodge, Sandy, Bedfordshire SG19 2DL.
*The British Trust for Ornithology*
Beech Grove, Tring, Hertfordshire.
*Watch*
22, The Green, Nettleham, Lincoln LN22 2RR.
(Watch runs a conservation club for children and schools.)
*Wildfowl and Wetlands Trust*
Slimbridge, Gloucestershire G12 7BT. (Write for information pack.)
*Council for Environmental Education*
School of Education, University of Reading,
London Road, Reading RG1 5AQ. (Information sheets available.)
*English Nature*
Northminster House, Peterborough PE1 1UA.
*Friends of the Earth* (UK)
26–28 Underwood Street, London N1 7JQ.
*Friends of the Earth* (Australia)
Chain Reaction Co-operative, P.O. Box 530E,
Melbourne, Victoria 3001.
*Friends of the Earth* (New Zealand)
P.O. Box 39—065, Aukland West.

## Identification guides

*The Pocket Oxford Book of Birds*
Bruce Campbell (OUP)
*The Observers' Book of Birds*
S. Vere Benson (Warne)
*A Field Guide to the Birds of Britain and Europe*
R.T. Peterson, G. Mountford and P.A.D. Hollom (Collins)
*The Usborne Nature Trail Book of Birdwatching* (Usborne).